The PERSONAL COOKBOOK

by Wendy Baker

GALLERY BOOKS

An Imprint of W. H. Smith Publishers, Inc.
112 Madison Avenue
New York, New York 10016

A FRIEDMAN GROUP BOOK

Published by GALLERY BOOKS
An imprint of W.H. Smith Publishers, Inc.
112 Madison Avenue
New York, New York 10016

ISBN 0-8317-8024-X

THE PERSONAL COOKBOOK
was produced and prepared by
Michael Friedman Publishing Group, Inc.
15 West 26th Street
New York, NY 10010

Illustrations: Susan Paradis

Typeset by BPE Graphics, Inc.
Printed and bound in Hong Kong by Leefung-Asco Printers Ltd.

CONTENTS

PART I
Basic Information

PART II
The Recipe Recordkeeper

CONTENTS

PART I
Basic Information

HERBS AND SPICES

It is best to buy herbs and spices whole. Just before using them crumble the leaves between your palms or grind them in a peppermill, coffee grinder, or pestle and mortar. Fresh-grinding is your assurance that the spices will taste their best. When shopping for herbs and spices, test with your eyes and nose. The greener the herb or the redder the spice means the better the quality. Spices that are bought in glass containers may have been exposed to fluorescent lights for months. Store your dried herbs away from heat in a dry, dark place and in airtight containers. Dried herbs rarely have a shelf life of longer than four months. If you want to add dry herbs to a sauce, put them in boiling water for less than a minute, strain, and pat dry. They'll be greener and more flavorful.

Allspice: berry of the allspice tree; native to the West Indies. Used principally in marinades, curries, and pickling fruits and vegetables. Good in pot roast, meat loaf, baked ham, stewed chicken, Swedish meatballs.

Anise: licoricelike flavor. Use sparingly, whole or crushed, in cookies, candies, fruit pies, compotes, applesauce, and spicecake. Adds flavor to warm milk or tea.

Basil: delicate and fragrant. Best with tomatoes, in cold salads, with seafood and cucumbers. Crush leaves just before adding.

Bay: has a refreshing, woodsy flavor. Excellent in soups, sauces, and stews. Use ½ leaf of the dried, 1 whole leaf of the fresh. Good with shrimp, crab, salmon, and lobster.

Caraway seed: characteristic flavor in German and Scandinavian bread. Used as a digestive aid. Add whole to potatoes, cabbage, beets, seasoned butters.

Cardamom: dried seed prevalent in Scandinavian pastries. Apropos in curry powders. For a different taste, try a bruised seed in a cup of after-dinner coffee.

Cayenne: a powder ground from the seeds and pods of various peppers grown in the Cayenne district of Africa. Good in soups, sauces, eggs, and meats. Use sparingly.

Celery seed: from the flowers of the celery plant. It can be used in any dish calling for fresh celery. Best with cheese and cocktail juices, pastries, and sandwich spreads.

Chili powder: made with the ground pods of Mexican peppers plus cumin, garlic, and oregano. Adds flavor spark to corn, beans, rice, creamed seafood, and spareribs.

Chives: grow these in your garden or windowbox. Best when eaten fresh. Perfect in salads, egg dishes, and with cottage cheese.

Cinnamon: from the bark of the cinnamon tree. Use in sweet potatoes, squash, rice pudding, ham, cocoa, poultry stuffing. Whole sticks or ground.

Cloves: strong spicy-sweet flavor. Perks up chocolate, rice, and tapioca puddings. Best in gingerbread, applesauce, spicecake, beef stew.

Coriander: good in soups, stews, curry dishes, and chili. Seeds are also used to flavor frankfurters, homemade butterscotch candy, and exotic dishes from North Africa.

Cumin: fairly well known in Mexican and eastern Indian cuisine. Rub the seeds briskly between palms and let them fall into stews.

Curry powder: generally a blend of 10 or more spices, including turmeric, cardamom, coriander, mustard, saffron, and allspice. Good with chicken, eggs, seafood salads.

Dill: the leaves, chopped, go well with poached salmon, sour cream and cucumbers, eggs, cheeses, and steak. Seeds are an ingredient for pickles, sauerkraut, and apple pie. Sprigs can be used as a garnish.

Fennel: all of the plant—seeds, bulb, stalk, and leaves—is edible. Tastes licoricelike. Use the same as anise or serve cold and eat raw like celery.

Garlic: one of the oldest cultivated plants. A whole bulb will enrich a stew or sauce, or the juice from a clove can flavor a salad dressing. Garlic butter enhances steaks, chops, bread, and spaghetti.

Ginger: pungent and zesty. It gives life to oriental dishes, meat, chicken, glazed carrots, fruit salad dressings, pie crusts.

Juniper berries: a bluish-purple dried fruit with a bittersweet taste. Good in marinades, sauerkraut, and game.

Leeks: popular in French cuisine. It is best in soups or stews, or cooked and served with lemon butter or vinaigrette sauce.

Mace: the outer coating of the nutmeg seed. Similar to nutmeg in taste and uses. It complements chocolate, cherry dishes, cakes, cookies, preserves.

Marjoram: part of the mint family. Spicy. Good substitute for sage. Best in food that requires lengthy cooking.

Mint: usually used fresh. When adding to cooked foods, put mint in shortly before food finishes cooking. Complements peas and carrots, salads, yogurt.

Mustard: the seeds are used for pickling and salad dressings. The powder is delicious in tuna, ham, seafood, egg, and potato salads, vegetable relish, lobster bisque. Can be made into a paste by adding water, milk, white wine, or beer and letting it stand for 15 minutes.

Nutmeg: freshly grated is much better than commercially ground. Use in eggnog, chocolate, coffee cake, puddings, sweet potatoes.

Oregano: indispensable in Italian, Mexican, and Spanish cooking. It is also known as wild marjoram. Good in any tomato sauce dish, with sharp cheeses, in guacamole.

Paprika: pleasantly mild to exceptionally hot. Ground powder of a pepper plant. The best quality is a vibrant red. Sprinkle on cottage cheese, sour cream, baked fish, cole slaw

Parsley: fresh is best, either curly or flat leaf. Can be used as a garnish. Brings out the flavor in food and other herbs.

Pepper: for the liveliest taste, buy whole black peppercorns and grind them in a mill. White pepper has the dark outer coating removed. It isn't quite as strong and is used in white sauces Red pepper flakes, used sparingly, add color and spark to pasta and eggs.

Pepper pods: not related to peppercorns. Ripe when they are red. Use in Indian and Mexican cuisine.

Poppy seed: these tiny seeds, not from the same plant that produces opium, taste similar to walnuts and are best in desserts, breads, pastries, and buttered noodles.

Rocket: otherwise known as arugula in Italian markets or roquette by the French. Use it as a salad green. Sharp, peppery.

Rosemary: spicy; comparable to mint. Use in dumplings and biscuits, lamb, pork, poultry, and oranges.

Saffron: from the stamen of the autumn crocus. Adds flavor to rice, Spanish, and Italian dishes. Buy it in threads for a fresher flavor and steep it in hot liquid before using.

Sage: slightly bitter. Use with a light touch and don't cook long. Best in stuffings for fish or fowl.

Savory: it is best with peas, beans, and lentils, chilled vegetable juices, and meat loaf. Both winter and summer varieties have a wonderful aroma, but the "winter" has a stronger taste.

Sesame seed: toasted nut flavor, intensifies when seeds are baked or roasted. Blend with butter to make a spread. Add to green salads and French dressing.

Shallots: member of the onion family. Similar to garlic and scallions. Exceptional in salad dressings, sprinkled on steaks.

Sorrel: sour-leaf version of spinach. Best with fish (fatty types), green salads, potato soup.

Tarragon: Indispensable. Can be used with poultry, fish, meat, salads, veal, and eggs.

Thyme: use sparingly as background flavor. Pungent. Combines well with bay leaf for soups and stuffings:

Turmeric: related to ginger. Use in curry dishes, pickle relishes. Substitute for saffron.

HELPFUL HINTS

When steaming potatoes, cover them with a cloth then put the lid on the pan. They will cook faster and have a firmer texture.

To make lettuce or salad greens crisp, add 1 tablespoon of vinegar to a pan of water and let them soak for 15 minutes.

A dash of salt added to coffee that has boiled or been reheated too often will freshen the taste.

Black walnuts ground in a blender will enhance the flavor of pumpkin pie.

Mayonnaise separates when it gets too cold. Keep it in the door shelf of the refrigerator.

When measuring syrup or molasses, rinse the spoon or cup in cold water first and the liquid won't adhere to the utensil.

Mustard added to a salad dressing will hold the oil and vinegar together.

To clean a cheese grater easily, rub it with raw potato after using it.

To prevent fruit juice from running over in pies, sprinkle a little baking soda over the fruit before laying on the top crust.

A teaspoon of wine added to waffle batter will keep it from sticking to the waffle iron.

To cool a hot dish in a hurry, place it in a pan of *salted* water.

The greener leaves on the outside of a head of lettuce contain more vitamins than the inside leaves, so try not to discard them.

If the outside of bread or cake gets too brown before the inside is cooked, place a pan of warm water on the oven rack above it.

A pinch of salt added to flour before it is mixed with the liquid will keep gravy from getting lumpy.

Potatoes will bake faster if they are soaked in hot water for 15 minutes or in salt water for 20 minutes.

To keep egg yolks, cover with cold water and keep in the refrigerator.

When doubling a recipe, don't automatically double the spices until sampling.

Iced tea and coffee are improved if the ice cubes are made of tea and coffee.

Pastry will be flakier if a few drops of vinegar are added to the iced water.

Clams will open easier if boiling water is poured over them.

Lemons and limes won't turn brown if they are stored in water in the refrigerator.

A sprinkling of flour or cornstarch on top of a cake will prevent the frosting from running off.

Salt toughens eggs, so add it to egg dishes only after they are cooked.

If citrus fruits are warmed in the oven for a few minutes, they will be juicier.

Dried fruit and nuts will sink to the bottom of a cake unless rolled in cake flour first.

Spinach will clean faster in warm water.

When cooking cabbage, cauliflower, broccoli, or brussels sprouts, put a slice of white bread into the saucepan and it will absorb the odor. Spoon it out before removing the vegetables.

To tenderize tough vegetables, simmer them in milk rather than water. Expect the milk to curdle slightly.

A dash of nutmeg in any white sauce is a spectacular addition.

When a custard pie shrinks away from the crust it has been baked in too hot an oven.

Fresh bread will retain its shape if sliced with a hot knife.

If an egg cracks while it is boiling, lower the heat and pour a lot of salt on the crack. This will seal the egg, keeping the white from leaking into the water.

Eggs that have been accidentally cracked in the carton can be boiled wrapped in greased paper, such as a butter wrapper, or in aluminum foil twisted closed at both ends.

Bake apples, stuffed green peppers, and tomatoes in a well-greased muffin tin and they will retain their shape better.

Add 1 teaspoon baking powder to potatoes that are to be mashed and then beat vigorously. They will be extra light and creamy.

For an easy-to-make fruit salad dressing, combine 1 teaspoon grated orange rind, ⅓ cup orange juice, and 1 cup sour cream.

To freshen Italian or French bread, sprinkle crust with cold water and place it in oven preheated to 350 degrees Fahrenheit for 10 minutes.

Mustard added to a dish at the beginning of its cooking time will be less pungent than if it is added at the end.

Bury a length of vanilla bean in an airtight jar of sugar and keep the vanilla sugar on hand for baking.

To get rid of bad kitchen odors, boil several cloves in 1 cup of water.

Chewing gum while peeling onions will prevent tears.

A pinch of salt added to whipped cream will make it whip faster.

To keep milk from sticking to a pan, rub the bottom of the pan with butter.

The leftover rinds of oranges, lemons, and grapefruit can be grated and stored in an airtight jar in the refrigerator to use in cakes and frostings.

To keep a cake from falling when it is taken out of the oven, fill the pan with batter, lift it up, and drop it suddenly on a table. This will release the air bubbles.

When making meringue shells, line the baking sheet with brown paper (from a bag) cut to fit.

To plump up dried-out raisins, wash and put them in a shallow dish, then bake, covered, at 350 degrees Fahrenheit until puffy.

To make a fine-textured cake, add a few drops of boiling water to the butter and sugar when creaming.

CALORIES

Almonds, 10 nuts	60
Anchovies, canned, 5 fillets	35
Apple juice, bottled, 1 cup	117
Apples, fresh with skin, 1 average	61
Applesauce, canned, ½ cup	116
Apricots	
fresh, 3 average	55
canned, heavy syrup, ½ cup	111
dried, ½ cup	169
Asparagus	
boiled, 4 spears	12
canned, ½ cup	25
frozen, 6 spears	23
Avocados	
California	185
Florida	196
Bacon, fried, 3 slices	86
Bagel, 1 medium	165
Bananas, 1 small	81
Bean curd, 1 cake	86
Bean sprouts, soy, raw, ½ cup	24
Beans, baked with pork, tomato sauce, ½ cup	156
Beans, green, boiled, ½ cup	16
Beans, lima	
boiled, ½ cup	95
canned, ½ cup	82
frozen, ½ cup	106
Beans, red kidney, canned, ½ cup	115
Beef, choice grade cuts	
brisket, lean only, braised, 4 oz	253
chuck, lean only, broiled, 4 oz	282
club steak, lean only, broiled, 4 oz	277
flank steak, lean, simmered, 4 oz	222
ground, lean, broiled, 4 oz	248
porterhouse, lean, broiled, 4 oz	254
rib, lean, roasted, 4 oz	273
round steak, lean, broiled, 4 oz	214
rump, lean, roasted, 4 oz	253
sirloin, lean, broiled, 4 oz	245
T-bone, lean, broiled, 4 oz	253
Beet greens, boiled, drained, ½ cup	13
Beets, boiled, sliced, ½ cup	33

Blueberries	
fresh, ½ cup	45
canned, syrup, ½ cup	126
frozen, sweetened, ½ cup	121
Bologna, all meat, 4 oz	315
Bouillon cube, 1	5
Brazil nuts, 3 large	90
Bread, 1 slice	
cracked wheat	60
French	44
Italian	28
pumpernickel	79
raisin	60
rye, whole wheat	56
white	63
Broccoli, boiled, ½ cup	20
Brussels sprouts, boiled, ½ cup	28
Butter, 1 tbsp	100
Cabbage	
red, raw, shredded, ½ cup	14
white, raw, shredded, ½ cup	11
white, boiled, ½ cup	16
Cantaloupe, ½ melon	58
Carrots	
raw, 1 average	21
boiled, ½ cup	23
Cashew nuts, roasted, salted, 4 oz	639
Catsup, 1 tbsp	16
Cauliflower	
raw, ½ cup	12
boiled, ½ cup	14
Caviar, sturgeon, granular, 1 oz	74
Celery, raw, 1 stalk	7
Cheese, 1 oz	
American processed, Edam	105
Camembert, mozzarella	85
cheddar	113
cottage, large curd, ½ cup	120
cottage, small curd, ½ cup	112
cream	106
fontina	114
Gouda	108
Gruyère	110
monterey Jack	103

Muenster	100
parmesan	111
parmesan, grated, 1 tbsp	23
provolone	99
ricotta	45
romano	110
romano, grated, 1 tbsp	30
Roquefort	105
Swiss	104
Chestnuts, 10	141
Chicken	
broiled, meat, no skin, 4 oz	154
roasted, meat and skin, 4 oz	283
stewed, meat only, ½ cup	135
Chili, canned, ½ cup	170
Chives, 1 tbsp	1
Chocolate, bitter or baking, unsweetened 1 oz	143
Clams, raw, 4 oz	92
Coconut, dried, unsweetened, shredded, 4 oz	751
Cod, broiled with butter, fillets, 4 oz	192
Cookies	
brownies, iced with nuts	103
chocolate chip	50
cream sandwich	49
fig bar	50
gingersnaps	29
graham cracker	55
macaroon	91
molasses	137
oatmeal and raisin	59
peanut sandwich	58
shortbread	37
vanilla wafer	19
Corn	
boiled on cob	70
boiled, kernels, ½ cup	69
canned, cream style, ½ cup	105
Cornmeal, ½ cup	217
Cornstarch, 1 tbsp	29
Crab, canned, 4 oz	115
Crackers	
cheese, 1 oz	136
Melba toast, 1	15
oyster, 1 oz	112
Ritz, 1	16
Rye-Krisp, 1; Triscuits, 1	21
Saltines, 1	12

Cranberry juice, bottled, 1 cup	164
Cranberry sauce, canned, ½ cup	202
Cream	
Half-and-Half, ½ cup	162
sour, ½ cup	243
whipping, ½ cup	419
Cucumber, 6 slices	4
Dates, 10	219
Duck, roasted, meat only, 4 oz	352
Eclair	239
Eggplant, boiled, diced, ½ cup	92
Eggs	
raw, whole	82
raw, white	17
raw, yolk	59
boiled, poached	82
fried	99
scrambled	111
Fat, vegetable, shortening, 1 tbsp	111
Figs	
fresh, 1 small	32
dried, 1 large	57
Finnan haddie, 4 oz	117
Flounder fillets, baked, 4 oz	229
Flour	
all-purpose, sifted, 1 cup	419
cake, sifted, 1 cup	349
wheat, sifted, 1 cup	405
Frankfurters, all-meat, 1	133
Ginger root, fresh, 1 oz	14
Goose, roasted, meat and skin, 4 oz	503
Grape juice	
bottled, 1 cup	167
frozen, 1 cup	133
Grapes	
Concord, 10	18
Thompson, 10	34
Grapefruit	
pink, ½ average	58
white, ½ average	54
Grapefruit juice, frozen, 1 cup	101
Ham, roasted, 4 oz	426
Herring, pickled, 4 oz	253
Honey, 1 tbsp	64
Honeydew melon, diced, ½ cup	28

Horseradish, prepared, 1 tbsp	6
Ice cream, rich, 16% fat, ½ cup	165
Ice cream bar, chocolate covered, 3 oz	162
Jams and preserves, 1 tbsp	54
Jellies, 1 tbsp	49
Kale, boiled, ½ cup	22
Lamb chop, broiled, 4 oz	341
Lard, 1 tbsp	117
Leeks, raw, 3 average	52
Lemon juice	
fresh, 1 tbsp	4
bottled, 1 cup	56
Lemonade, frozen, diluted, 1 cup	107
Lemons, 1 average	20
Lentils, cooked, 1 cup	212
Lettuce	
Boston, 1 head	23
Iceberg, 1 head	70
Romaine, 3 leaves	5
Liver	
beef, fried, 4 oz	260
calf, fried, 4 oz	296
chicken, simmered, 4 oz	187
Liverwurst, 4 oz	362
Lobster, cooked, meat only, 4 oz	108
Macaroni, boiled, ½ cup	96
Mangoes, 1	152
Marmalade, 1 tbsp	51
Milk	
whole, 1 cup	159
buttermilk, 1 cup; skim, 1 cup	88
sweetened, condensed, 1 cup	982
evaporated, 1 cup	345
Muffin	
corn	130
English	140
Mussels, raw, 4 oz	130
Mustard, prepared, 1 tbsp	4
Nectarines, 1	88
Noodles, egg, cooked, ½ cup	100
Oil	
corn, safflower, sesame, 1 tbsp	120
olive, peanut, 1 tbsp	119
Okra, boiled, 10 pods	41
Olives, green, 10 large	45

Orange juice	
fresh, 1 cup	120
frozen, diluted, 1 cup	112
Oranges, 1	63
Oysters	
east coast, 2–3	19
west coast, 6–9	218
Pancakes, plain, buttermilk, 4 in	61
Papaya, 1	119
Parsley, 1 tbsp	2
Parsnips, boiled, mashed, ½ cup	70
Pâté de foie gras, 1 oz	131
Peaches	
fresh, 1	38
canned, syrup, ½ cup	100
dried, ½ cup	210
Peanut butter, commercial, 1 tbsp	94
Peanuts	
raw, shelled, 4 oz	640
roasted, halves, ½ cup	421
Pears	
Bartlett	100
Bosc	86
D'Anjou	122
canned in syrup, 4 oz	87
dried, ½ cup	241
Peas, boiled, ½ cup	57
Pecans, 10	62
Peppers, green, raw, ½ cup	17
Peppers, red, raw, chopped, ½ cup	24
Pickle relish, 1 tbsp	17
Pickles	
dill, 1	15
sour, 1	14
sweet, 1	22
Pineapple	
fresh, diced, ½ cup	41
canned in syrup, 4 oz	84
Pineapple juice, canned, 1 cup	138
Pistachio nuts, shelled, ½ cup	372
Plums, 1	66
Pomegranates, 1	97
Popcorn	
popped plain, 1 cup	23
oil and salt, 1 cup	41
Pork chop, broiled, 4 oz	308

Potato chips, 10	114
Potatoes	
baked in skin	145
boiled, peeled	88
french fried	137
mashed with milk, butter, ½ cup	99
Potatoes, sweet	
baked in skin	161
candied, 1	176
Pretzels, 1 oz	111
Prune juice, bottled, 1 cup	197
Prunes, dried, 1	16
Pumpkin, canned, ½ cup	41
Radishes, raw, 10	14
Raisins, 4 oz	328
Raspberries	
black, fresh, ½ cup	49
red, fresh, ½ cup	35
Rhubarb, cooked, sweetened, ½ cup	191
Rice, cooked, long-grain	
brown, ½ cup	116
white, ½ cup	112
Rolls	
dinner	83
hamburger/frankfurter	119
Kaiser	156
raisin	78
sweet	89
Salad dressings, 1 tbsp	
blue cheese	76
French	66
Italian	83
mayonnaise	101
Thousand Island	80
Salami, 1 slice	68
Salmon	
steak, broiled, 4 oz	207
canned, pink, 4 oz	160
smoked, 4 oz	200
Sauces	
soy, 1 tbsp	74
Worcestershire, 1 tbsp	15
Sausage, pork	
1 link	62
Shrimp, fresh, breaded, fried, 4 oz	255
Soda, 1 cup	
club	0
cola	96

cream	105
ginger ale	76
root beer	100
7-Up	97
tonic	76
Spaghetti	
boiled, ½ cup	96
Spinach, boiled, ½ cup	21
Squash, summer	
yellow, boiled, ½ cup	14
zucchini, boiled, ½ cup	14
Squash	
acorn, baked, ½ squash	86
butternut, baked, ½ cup	70
Strawberries	
fresh, ½ cup	28
frozen, sliced, sweetened, ½ cup	139
Sugar	
brown, ½ cup	411
brown, 1 tbsp	52
granulated, ½ cup	385
granulated, 1 tbsp	46
powdered, ½ cup	231
powdered, 1 tbsp	31
maple, 4 oz	395
Swordfish, broiled, 4 oz	186
Syrup	
corn, 1 tbsp	58
molasses, 1 tbsp	43
Tangerine, 1	39
Tomato juice	
bottled, 1 cup	46
paste, ½ cup	108
Tomatoes, raw, 1 average	20
Tuna, in oil, drained, ½ cup	158
Turkey	
dark meat, roasted, 4 oz	230
light meat, roasted, 4 oz	200
Veal, loin, broiled, 4 oz	245
Vinegar, cider, 1 tbsp	2
Walnuts, English, 10	322
Water chestnuts, raw, whole, 5–7	79
Watercress, raw, ½ cup	4
Watermelon, 1 average wedge	111
Wheat germ, 1 tbsp	23
Yeast, brewer's dry, 1 oz	80
Yogurt, plain, whole milk	152

GLOSSARY

al dente: an Italian phrase that means "to the tooth" and refers to cooking pasta tender but firm.

amandine: made or served with almonds.

arrowroot: an American tropical plant whose root yields a nutritive starch that can be used as a thickening agent.

aspic: a jelly made from stock or tomato juice and gelatin.

bard: to tie a thin layer of fat around lean meats to keep them from drying out in cooking.

beard: to cut the hairy fibers off unshucked mussels.

béarnaise: a rich egg sauce flavored with wine and herbs.

béchamel: a basic white sauce.

bisque: a creamy soup with a shellfish base.

blanc, au: poached or simmered and served in a white sauce.

bordelaise: a basic brown sauce with bordeaux wine for part of the liquid.

bouillabaisse: a stew of different kinds of fish and shellfish.

bouquet garni: a small bunch of dried or fresh herbs tied in cheesecloth and used to flavor stocks and stews; it consists of parsley, thyme, tarragon, bay leaf, marjoram, and chervil.

bourguignonne: a rich sauce of burgundy wine, braised onions, and mushrooms.

braise: to brown in fat then cook, covered, on the stove top or in the oven with a small amount of liquid and seasoning.

brine: to preserve in a strong salt solution, or the solution itself.

bruise: to crush partially in a pestle and mortar to release flavor, as with cardamom, garlic cloves, or peppercorns.

butterfly: to split food down the center not quite all the way so the two halves open like butterfly wings.

caramelize: to melt granulated sugar in a heavy saucepan over very low heat until sugar is liquid and brown.

chapon: a cube or chunk of bread rubbed with oil and garlic and tossed with salad to impart a subtle flavor. Discard before serving. An alternative method: rub the salad bowl with the chapon before greens are added.

chateaubriand: a thick fillet of beef.

clarify: to make a cloudy liquid clear.

coat a spoon: a doneness test for sauces, custards, and soups. A spoon dipped into a cream soup should have a thin film when withdrawn. Dipped into a sauce made for covering food, it should emerge with a thick coating.

coddle: to poach in water just below the boiling point.

compote: fruits stewed in a light syrup.

coquille: a scallop or shell, or a dish served in shells.

court bouillon: liquid in which fish is cooked, containing water, white wine, vegetables, herbs, salt, and pepper.

crimp: to seal the edge of a pie or pastry with an attractive edge.

cut and fold: to cut through a mixture with a spoon or spatula, turn, and mix from the bottom.

cut in shortening: to mix shortening into dry ingredients with fingers, two knives, or pastry blender, until it is mealy.

deglaze: after meat, fish, or poultry has been roasted or sautéed, and the pan degreased, liquid is poured into the pan and all flavorful cooking juices are scraped up and simmered. It can be used as a sauce by itself or in addition to others.

dredge: to coat with seasoned flour, bread or cracker crumbs, or sugar.

drizzle: to sprinkle drops of butter, syrup, or sauce over the surface of food in a fine stream.

duchesse: potatoes mashed with cream, enriched with egg yolk, and pressed out through a pastry tube.

dust: to coat lightly with flour, confectioner's sugar, or any powder mixture. More lightly coated than dredged.

flan: open custard or fruit tart.

florentine: food served with or on a bed of spinach, often creamed.

fluff: to fork up until light and fluffy.

flute: to make a decorative edge on pies, pastries, or to cut mushrooms or other small vegetables into scalloped shapes.

fricassee: a stew of chicken, rabbit, or veal in white sauce.

frizzle: to fry thinly sliced meat at intense heat until crisp and curled.

glaze: to cover food with glossy coating, syrup, vinegar, aspic, jellies.

gratiné: to brown the top of a sauced dish under the broiler. Bread crumbs, grated cheese, and butter help form crust.

leaven: to lighten the texture and increase the volume of breads, cakes, cookies by using baking soda, powder, or yeast.

meunière, à la: sautéed food, most often fish, served with butter and lemon sauce.

mince: to chop very fine. After chopping roughly with one hand on top of the blade and the other on the handle, rock blade back and forth from one end of pile to the other to chop into desired sized bits.

mornay: a rich sauce with melted cheese.

nap: to cover food with a cream sauce which is thick enough so that it doesn't hide outline of food.

parboil: to cook briefly in boiling water or seasoned liquid or in a skillet over direct heat with little fat.

pâte: a paste, dough, or frying batter.

pâté: a pie or spread containing ground meat, fish, or poultry and served cold.

pilaf: a dish flavored with saffron, turmeric and meat, poultry, or fish.

praline: flavored with browned almonds and browned in syrup.

purée: to grind a paste, to mash to a smooth blend.

ragout: a rich, brown stew with meat and vegetables.

refresh: plunge hot food into ice-cold water in order to cool it immediately, stop the cooking process, and preserve color.

render: to heat lard or other animal fat so that it melts away from connective tissue and turns into a pure, smooth, and creamy substance. Use double boiler, press down on fat with spoon with cooking. Perfect for pastry.

scallop: the verb means to bake with a sauce or cream.

score: to make shallow cuts in long lines in the meat and fish to keep them from curling up when broiled.

shirr: to cook whole eggs in a small baking dish with cream and often a topping of bread crumbs, buttered.

sorbet: a partially frozen ice made of water, fruit, and liqueur.

spin a thread: to cook a syrup to 238 degrees, at which point a thin brittle thread forms when a spoon is taken out of the boiling liquid.

stiff but not dry: describes beaten egg whites that stand up in stiff, moist peaks.

stock: the broth strained from stewed or boiled meats, seafood, poultry, or vegetables.

stud: to insert whole cloves or slivers of garlic into the surface of food.

swirl: to whirl liquid gently in a pan.

truss: to bind a bird into a compact shape before roasting.

SUBSTITUTIONS

allspice, 1 teaspoon = ½ teaspoon cinnamon plus ⅛ teaspoon ground cloves

baking powder, 1 teaspoon = 1 teaspoon baking soda plus 1 teaspoon cream of tartar, or ¼ teaspoon baking soda plus ½ cup buttermilk or sour milk (to replace ½ cup of liquid)

cake flour, 1 cup = 1 cup all-purpose flour minus 2 tablespoons

chicken broth, 1 cup canned = 1 cube or 1 envelope plus 2 cups boiling water

chocolate, 1 square unsweetened = 3 tablespoons cocoa plus 1 tablespoon butter or margarine

cornstarch, 1 tablespoon = 2 tablespoons flour or 4 teaspoons quick-cooking tapioca

corn syrup, 1½ cups = 1 cup sugar plus ½ cup water

egg, 1 whole = 2 egg yolks plus 1 tablespoon water

flour, 1 cup presifted = 1 cup plus 2 tablespoons cake flour

garlic, 1 clove = ⅛ teaspoon garlic powder

ginger, 1 tablespoon raw = ⅛ teaspoon ginger powder

herbs, 1 tablespoon fresh = 1 teaspoon dried

honey, ⅔ cup = 1 cup sugar plus ⅓ cup water

Italian seasoning, 1 teaspoon = ¼ teaspoon each of oregano, basil, thyme, rosemary plus dash of cayenne

lemon juice, 1 teaspoon = ½ teaspoon vinegar

buttermilk or sour milk, 1 cup = 1 tablespoon lemon juice or vinegar plus milk to make 1 cup (let stand 5 minutes)

whole milk, 1 cup = ½ cup evaporated milk plus ½ cup water or 1 cup reconstituted nonfat dry milk plus 2½ teaspoons butter or margarine

mushrooms, ½ pound = 4 ounces canned mushrooms

mustard, 1 teaspoon dry = 1 tablespoon prepared

onion, 1 small = 1 tablespoon instant minced onion

oregano, 1 teaspoon = 1 teaspoon marjoram

raisins, ½ cup = ½ cup dried cut prunes

shrimp, 1 pound shelled, deveined, cooked = 5 ounces canned shrimp

Tabasco, a few drops = dash of cayenne pepper

tomatoes, 1 cup canned = 1⅓ cup fresh tomatoes simmered 10 minutes

tomato juice, 1 cup = ½ cup tomato sauce plus ½ cup water

Worcestershire, 1 teaspoon = 1 teaspoon bottled steak sauce

yeast, 1 cake compressed = 1 package or 2 teaspoons active dry yeast

EQUIVALENTS AND METRIC CONVERSIONS

LIQUID MEASURE EQUIVALENTS

3 teaspoons = 1 tablespoon

2 tablespoons = 1 fluid ounce

4 tablespoons = ¼ cup = 2 fluid ounces

5 tablespoons + 1 teaspoon = ⅓ cup = 2⅔ ounces

8 tablespoons = ½ cup = 4 fluid ounces

10 tablespoons = 2 teaspoons = ⅔ cup

12 tablespoons = ¾ cup

16 tablespoons = 1 cup = 8 fluid ounces

2 cups = 16 fluid ounces = 1 pint

4 cups = 32 fluid ounces = 1 quart

8 cups = 64 fluid ounces = ½ gallon

4 quarts = 128 fluid ounces = 1 gallon

METRIC CONVERSION TABLE

To change	To	Multiply by
teaspoons	milliliters	5
tablespoons	milliliters	15
fluid ounces	milliliters	30
ounces	grams	28
cups	liters	0.24
pints	liters	0.47
quarts	liters	0.95
gallons	liters	3.8
pounds	kilograms	0.45
Fahrenheit	Celsius	$5/9$ after subtracting 32

PART II
The Recipe Recordkeeper

HORS D'OEUVRE AND APPETIZERS

Recipe

Source _____ Serves _____

Ingredients _____

_____

_____

_____

_____

Directions _____

_____

_____

_____

_____

_____

_____

_____

_____

_____

_____

_____

_____

_____

_____

Recipe _____

Source _____ Serves _____

Ingredients _____

_____

_____

_____

_____

_____

Directions _____

_____

_____

_____

_____

_____

_____

_____

_____

_____

_____

_____

_____

Recipe

Source _____ Serves _____

Ingredients _____

_____

_____

_____

_____

_____

_____

Directions _____

_____

_____

_____

_____

_____

_____

_____

_____

_____

_____

_____

_____

_____

Recipe _____

Source _____ Serves _____

Ingredients _____

_____

_____

_____

_____

_____

_____

Directions _____

_____

_____

_____

_____

_____

_____

_____

_____

_____

_____

_____

_____

_____

_____

Recipe

Source _____ Serves _____

Ingredients _____

_____

_____

_____

_____

_____

_____

Directions _____

_____

_____

_____

_____

_____

_____

_____

_____

_____

_____

_____

_____

_____

Recipe

Source _____ Serves _____

Ingredients _____

_____

_____

_____

_____

_____

_____

Directions _____

_____

_____

_____

_____

_____

_____

_____

_____

_____

_____

_____

_____

_____

_____

SALADS

Recipe _____

Source _____ Serves _____

Ingredients _____

_____

_____

_____

_____

Directions _____

_____

_____

_____

_____

_____

_____

_____

_____

_____

_____

_____

_____

_____

_____

_____

Recipe

Source _____ Serves _____

Ingredients _____

_____

_____

_____

_____

_____

_____

Directions _____

_____

_____

_____

_____

_____

_____

_____

_____

_____

_____

_____

_____

_____

_____

Recipe

Source _____ Serves _____

Ingredients _____

_____

_____

_____

_____

_____

_____

Directions _____

_____

_____

_____

_____

_____

_____

_____

_____

_____

_____

_____

_____

_____

Recipe

Source _____ Serves _____

Ingredients _____

_____

_____

_____

_____

_____

Directions _____

_____

_____

_____

_____

_____

_____

_____

_____

_____

_____

_____

_____

_____

SOUPS AND STOCKS

Recipe

Source _____ Serves _____

Ingredients _____

_____

_____

_____

_____

Directions _____

_____

_____

_____

_____

_____

_____

_____

_____

_____

_____

_____

_____

_____

_____

Recipe

Source _____ Serves _____

Ingredients _____

_____

_____

_____

_____

_____

Directions _____

_____

_____

_____

_____

_____

_____

_____

_____

_____

_____

_____

_____

_____

Recipe

Source _____ Serves _____

Ingredients _____

_____

_____

_____

_____

_____

Directions _____

_____

_____

_____

_____

_____

_____

_____

_____

_____

_____

_____

_____

_____

Recipe

Source _____ Serves _____

Ingredients _____

_____

_____

_____

_____

_____

Directions _____

_____

_____

_____

_____

_____

_____

_____

_____

_____

_____

_____

_____

_____

_____

PASTA AND RICES

Recipe

Source _____ Serves _____

Ingredients _____
_____
_____
_____
_____

Directions _____
_____
_____
_____
_____
_____
_____
_____
_____
_____
_____
_____
_____
_____
_____
_____

Recipe _____

Source _____ Serves _____

Ingredients _____

_____

_____

_____

_____

_____

_____

Directions _____

_____

_____

_____

_____

_____

_____

_____

_____

_____

_____

_____

_____

_____

_____

_____

Recipe

Source _____ Serves _____

Ingredients _____

_____

_____

_____

_____

_____

_____

Directions _____

_____

_____

_____

_____

_____

_____

_____

_____

_____

_____

_____

_____

_____

_____

Recipe

Source _____ Serves _____

Ingredients _____

_____

_____

_____

_____

_____

Directions _____

_____

_____

_____

_____

_____

_____

_____

_____

_____

_____

_____

_____

_____

EGGS

Recipe

Source_____ Serves_____

Ingredients_____

_____

_____

_____

_____

Directions_____

_____

_____

_____

_____

_____

_____

_____

_____

_____

_____

_____

_____

_____

_____

_____

Use This Space For Clippings

Use This Space For Clippings

Recipe

Source _____ Serves _____

Ingredients _____

_____

_____

_____

_____

_____

_____

Directions _____

_____

_____

_____

_____

_____

_____

_____

_____

_____

_____

_____

_____

_____

_____

Recipe _____

Source _____ Serves _____

Ingredients _____

_____

_____

_____

_____

_____

_____

Directions _____

_____

_____

_____

_____

_____

_____

_____

_____

_____

_____

_____

_____

_____

_____

_____

VEGETABLES

Recipe

Source _____ Serves _____

Ingredients _____

_____

_____

_____

_____

Directions _____

_____

_____

_____

_____

_____

_____

_____

_____

_____

_____

_____

_____

_____

_____

_____

Recipe

Source _____ Serves _____

Ingredients _____

_____

_____

_____

_____

_____

Directions _____

_____

_____

_____

_____

_____

_____

_____

_____

_____

_____

_____

_____

_____

_____

Recipe

Source _____ Serves _____

Ingredients _____

_____

_____

_____

_____

_____

Directions _____

_____

_____

_____

_____

_____

_____

_____

_____

_____

_____

_____

_____

Recipe

Source _____ Serves _____

Ingredients _____

_____

_____

_____

_____

_____

Directions _____

_____

_____

_____

_____

_____

_____

_____

_____

_____

_____

_____

_____

_____

_____

SAUCES, DRESSINGS, AND STUFFINGS

Recipe _____

Source _____ Serves _____

Ingredients _____
_____
_____
_____
_____

Directions _____
_____
_____
_____
_____
_____
_____
_____
_____
_____
_____
_____
_____
_____
_____
_____

Recipe

Source _____ Serves _____

Ingredients _____

_____

_____

_____

_____

_____

Directions _____

_____

_____

_____

_____

_____

_____

_____

_____

_____

_____

_____

_____

_____

Recipe

Source _____ Serves _____

Ingredients _____

_____

_____

_____

_____

_____

Directions _____

_____

_____

_____

_____

_____

_____

_____

_____

_____

_____

_____

_____

_____

_____

Recipe

Source _____ Serves _____

Ingredients _____

_____

_____

_____

_____

_____

_____

Directions _____

_____

_____

_____

_____

_____

_____

_____

_____

_____

_____

_____

_____

_____

FISH

Recipe _____

Source _____ Serves _____

Ingredients _____

_____

_____

_____

_____

Directions _____

_____

_____

_____

_____

_____

_____

_____

_____

_____

_____

_____

_____

_____

Recipe _____

Source _____ Serves _____

Ingredients _____

_____

_____

_____

_____

_____

_____

Directions _____

_____

_____

_____

_____

_____

_____

_____

_____

_____

_____

_____

_____

_____

Recipe _____

Source _____ Serves _____

Ingredients _____

_____

_____

_____

_____

_____

Directions _____

_____

_____

_____

_____

_____

_____

_____

_____

_____

_____

_____

_____

_____

Recipe

Source _____ Serves _____

Ingredients _____

_____

_____

_____

_____

_____

_____

Directions _____

_____

_____

_____

_____

_____

_____

_____

_____

_____

_____

_____

_____

_____

POULTRY AND GAMEBIRDS

Recipe _____

Source _____ Serves _____

Ingredients _____

_____

_____

_____

_____

Directions _____

_____

_____

_____

_____

_____

_____

_____

_____

_____

_____

_____

_____

_____

_____

Recipe _____

Source _____ Serves _____

Ingredients _____

_____

_____

_____

_____

_____

Directions _____

_____

_____

_____

_____

_____

_____

_____

_____

_____

_____

_____

_____

_____

_____

_____

Recipe _____

Source _____ Serves _____

Ingredients _____

_____

_____

_____

_____

_____

Directions _____

_____

_____

_____

_____

_____

_____

_____

_____

_____

_____

_____

_____

Recipe

Source _____ Serves _____

Ingredients _____

_____

_____

_____

_____

_____

Directions _____

_____

_____

_____

_____

_____

_____

_____

_____

_____

_____

_____

_____

_____

_____

Recipe

Source _____ Serves _____

Ingredients _____

_____

_____

_____

_____

_____

Directions _____

_____

_____

_____

_____

_____

_____

_____

_____

_____

_____

_____

_____

_____

Use This Space For Clippings

MEAT

Recipe _____

Source _____ Serves _____

Ingredients _____

_____

_____

_____

_____

Directions _____

_____

_____

_____

_____

_____

_____

_____

_____

_____

_____

_____

_____

_____

_____

_____

Recipe

Source _____ Serves _____

Ingredients _____

_____

_____

_____

_____

_____

_____

Directions _____

_____

_____

_____

_____

_____

_____

_____

_____

_____

_____

_____

_____

_____

_____

_____

Recipe

Source _____ Serves _____

Ingredients _____

_____

_____

_____

_____

_____

Directions _____

_____

_____

_____

_____

_____

_____

_____

_____

_____

_____

_____

_____

_____

Recipe

Source _____ Serves _____

Ingredients _____

_____

_____

_____

_____

_____

Directions _____

_____

_____

_____

_____

_____

_____

_____

_____

_____

_____

_____

_____

_____

_____

Recipe

Source _____ Serves _____

Ingredients _____

_____

_____

_____

_____

_____

_____

Directions _____

_____

_____

_____

_____

_____

_____

_____

_____

_____

_____

_____

_____

_____

Recipe

Source _____ Serves _____

Ingredients _____

_____

_____

_____

_____

_____

_____

Directions _____

_____

_____

_____

_____

_____

_____

_____

_____

_____

_____

_____

_____

_____

_____

_____

Use This Space For Clippings

Recipe _____

Source _____ Serves _____

Ingredients _____

_____

_____

_____

_____

_____

_____

Directions _____

_____

_____

_____

_____

_____

_____

_____

_____

_____

_____

_____

_____

_____

_____

BREADS

Recipe _____

Source _____ Serves _____

Ingredients _____

_____

_____

_____

_____

Directions _____

_____

_____

_____

_____

_____

_____

_____

_____

_____

_____

_____

_____

_____

Recipe _____

Source _____ Serves _____

Ingredients _____

_____

_____

_____

_____

_____

_____

Directions _____

_____

_____

_____

_____

_____

_____

_____

_____

_____

_____

_____

_____

_____

_____

_____

Recipe

Source _____ Serves _____

Ingredients _____
_____
_____
_____
_____
_____

Directions _____
_____
_____
_____
_____
_____
_____
_____
_____
_____
_____
_____
_____
_____
_____

Recipe

Source _____ Serves _____

Ingredients _____

_____

_____

_____

_____

_____

_____

Directions _____

_____

_____

_____

_____

_____

_____

_____

_____

_____

_____

_____

_____

_____

_____

PIES, PASTRIES, CAKES, AND COOKIES

Recipe

Source _____   Serves _____

Ingredients _____
_____
_____
_____
_____

Directions _____
_____
_____
_____
_____
_____
_____
_____
_____
_____
_____
_____
_____
_____
_____

Recipe

Source _____ Serves _____

Ingredients _____

_____

_____

_____

_____

_____

_____

Directions _____

_____

_____

_____

_____

_____

_____

_____

_____

_____

_____

_____

_____

_____

_____

Recipe

Source _____ Serves _____

Ingredients _____

_____

_____

_____

_____

_____

Directions _____

_____

_____

_____

_____

_____

_____

_____

_____

_____

_____

_____

_____

Recipe

Source _____ Serves _____

Ingredients _____

_____

_____

_____

_____

_____

Directions _____

_____

_____

_____

_____

_____

_____

_____

_____

_____

_____

_____

_____

_____

Spiced Dutch Apples
Recipe

Source _____ Serves _____

Ingredients

15-20 sweet APPLES (GOLDEN)	- PEEL and CORE APPLES
COCONUT OIL	- COOK APPLES IN SAUCE PAN w/
WATER	OIL AND WATER
CLOVE	- ADD RAISINS
MACE	- ADD SALT AND SPICES
CINNAMON	
GINGER	- COOK UNTIL TENDER
SALT	
RAISINS	
NUTMEG	

Directions Pumpkin Spice Custard

1 CAN PUMPKIN	- BLOOM GELATIN IN COCONUT CREAM
1 CAN COCONUT CREAM	- HEAT ALL INGREDIENTS
1 TSP VANILLA	EXCEPT PUMPKIN IN SAUCEPAN
4 TSP GELATIN	OVER MEDIUM HEAT UNTIL JUST
23 TBS HONEY	STARTING TO SIMMER AND
3 TBS MAPLE SYRUP	GELATIN IS DISSOLVED.
1 TSP CINNAMON	- ADD PUMPKIN, REMOVE FROM
2 TSP GINGER	HEAT. POUR INTO DEEP DISH.
1/2 TSP MACE	REFRIGERATE UNTIL SET,
1/4 TSP CLOVES	≈4 HOURS.
1/4 TSP SALT	

Use This Space For Clippings

ICINGS, CANDIES, TOPPINGS, AND GLAZES

Recipe _____

Source _____ Serves _____

Ingredients _____

_____

_____

_____

_____

Directions _____

_____

_____

_____

_____

_____

_____

_____

_____

_____

_____

_____

_____

_____

_____

Use This Space For Clippings

Recipe _____

Source _____ Serves _____

Ingredients _____

_____

_____

_____

_____

_____

_____

Directions _____

_____

_____

_____

_____

_____

_____

_____

_____

_____

_____

_____

_____

_____

Recipe

Source _____ Serves _____

Ingredients _____

_____

_____

_____

_____

_____

_____

Directions _____

_____

_____

_____

_____

_____

_____

_____

_____

_____

_____

_____

_____

_____

_____